WHEN LOVERS DISCOVER EACH OTHER

Exploring the Depths of Love

Reginald Reaves

Published by Reginald Reaves in association with Faith and Family Restoration, a ministry of ReginaldReaves.com

ISBN: 9798563376540

Printed in the United States of America

This book is dedicated to my beautiful wife,
Katrina,
I have written this book because of you and the
love that we share. I'm enjoying our love journey,
discovering daily the sweetness of you. I laugh when
I think about the first time, I called you while on
break at work, and all through our conversation,
I was tasting sugar. It was a sign to me, that this
young lady is sweet! We're not perfect, but we
are just right for each other. You helped to pull
this project together and gave me wise counsel
throughout. Thank you for loving me;
I'll love you all my days.

To my daughters Brielle and Thalia,
You fill our home and my heart with so much love
and joy. Thank you for inspiring me to be all that
God is calling me to be.

To my parents, Bishop Alfred, and Lady Marlene
Reaves,
Your love for God and each other are a shining
example of love, faith, and steadfast commitment.
Spanning over 60 years together in marriage and
ministry, you are living proof that God is faithful.

From the heart and hand of Reginald Reaves

CONTENTS

INTRODUCTION

Marriages don't have to stale or run out of the passion that was present during the early stages of the relationship. Too often, that's the case when it comes to marriages and couples fall victim to the routine and repetitive nature of married life. Between family and work obligations, there may be only a fraction of time remaining for romance. Couples that can squeeze in a "date night" often spend much of that time wondering, "Are the kids alright with the babysitter?" and "How much time is left before they have to jump back into the hustle and bustle of life?"

For many Christian couples, a considerable amount of time is allotted for church and ministry, further eating into the time that might be spent on developing your relationship. Before long, a mindset develops that aids loss of interest in romance and tiredness, boredom and frustration can set in and the couple may begin to drift apart. When there's distance between husband and wife, it prevents them from enjoying the intimacy that God intends for couples to have and opens the door to temptation and trouble. Whatever they're missing from the marriage, they begin to look for it elsewhere when they no longer feel that closeness with their spouse. This scenario has played out many times and is currently threatening countless marriages. This book will address these issues and others in a brief but comprehensive way, giving insight into how single people should approach dating, leading to marriage; and how those that are married can grow together in a lifetime of love, pleasure, and discovery. We will examine the scriptures to see God's idea of intimacy, how our hearts can communicate on the deepest level, and how to mutually provide a safe place in your marriage that will encourage your spouse to unveil to you the essence of their being.

So many only feel worth and significance when they are in a romantic relationship. For them, to be alone is depressing, and it makes them restless, desiring to be involved with someone. This becomes the pursuit that occupies much of their thinking. We all have a natural need to be loved and to give love. Our identity, however, should be realized before we can truly be the person that God intends for us to be in a loving marriage. Once you know who you are and where you fit in God's purpose, you will be positioned to love that special person that God is preparing for you.

The wounds we received from bad relationships can distort our perception of who we are, what we want/need, or what's best for us. The hurtful things that were said to us or what we said to others in previous relationships echo in the chambers of our mind, and many of the painful episodes from our past attempts at love are replayed in each new relationship. It's necessary to grow out of where we've been, extracting the lessons, applying them to now, and finding yourself in God's grand plan.

There are arguments that some make against getting married that stem from failed relationships or their contempt for the thought of being with the same person for the rest of their life. It seems boring and redundant to them to wake up to the same person, day after day. Society has us so accustomed to variety, and we feel such a need to change, that we often see that approach applied to relationships. From our devices to our network subscriptions, it's all about change, renew, update, upgrade, and the list goes on. When that kind of thinking is applied to relationships, new and different people come parading in and out of your life, scattering your soul, and the residue from each relationship is collected and stored in your emotions. You go into the next relationship with the baggage that was dumped on you from the last, and that cycle is repeated, like an unwanted cable TV plan is (automatically) renewed.

Even worse, some approach their relationships open to the idea of being involved with multiple people at the same time (multi-dating), seeking to piece together certain traits from each person to get all the qualities that they desire. The excitement of having several people in your life gives a false reading of the true state of your heart; that thrill is nothing more than a short-lived pleasure that prevents you from finding love which is really what you were made for. Being involved with numerous people simultaneously doesn't allow you to get a true assessment on one person because you're crowding your mind and emotions with multiple people. Like a reality TV show, many are involved with people as if they were contestants that are competing to win them over, trying not to be eliminated. As a result, some get comfortable simply dating and becoming anti-marriage. You subscribe to the opinion that marriage is restrictive, confining, and dull. The truth is that marriage is designed by God Himself to be a refuge, a place where the couple can uncover their hearts in full disclosure and be safe in doing so.

Marriage is a voyage into the immeasurable oceans of love and into each other, as you both learn to appreciate the life you share together. God says of marriage,

And they two shall be one flesh Gen. 2:24.

In these words (shall be), we see a process. Saying "I do" to each other doesn't automatically make you one; it simply initiates the lifelong endeavor of blending your lives. The very next words that follow the statement of Adam and Eve becoming one are

And they were both naked, the man and his wife, and were not ashamed Gen. 2:25.

The importance of this verse is that it shows God's design for a man and his wife to have true intimacy. It is a comfort level of being able to show yourself to the person that you have pledged to be with for a lifetime. Not just physical nakedness but allowing your spouse to see inside your heart.

When Lovers Discover Each Other will bring couples to the pivotal moment of recognition that marriage is a joint journey through life where practicing humility, patience, and forgiveness will increase the depth of your love. Those that are looking for love will understand the mindset that is needed to go into a relationship, equipped with insights as to what God has in mind concerning marriage. Troubled marriages will be encouraged to hope and believe again in the unfailing love of God. His love is a gift to be enjoyed between husband and wife in all its mystery and surprise.

SECTION 1:
LOOKING

Looking

The top selling book genre is romance. More than horror books and science fiction novels; more than inspirational books or even crime/mystery novels, the romance category outsells them all. Many love to read about relationships and to have their heart-strings pulled in different directions by the complicated, steamy situations that fills the pages of these novels. Whether it's because people can relate to what they're reading or because they are entertained by it, these books continue to be consumed on a large scale.

The Bible is the most read book of all time. It continues to be the most recognizable book that has ever been published. Although it consists of stories, historical accounts, prophecies, prayers, teachings, and many other wise, instructional writings that we believe are inspired by God Himself; it also lays bare what love should look like in marriage, even exposing the ugliness of unfaithfulness. Many that read the Bible, are looking for answers to the questions of life. They may be looking for direction, their purpose, or the meaning of our existence. At some point in our lives, we all ponder these things and seek to find answers. The Bible, which is the word of God, provides answers. It is a love story that spans from eternity, through time, and into an everlasting age of peace and joy. It is God's love letter to you and me.

In this section of the book, what I hope to convey is the great need to grow in our relationship with the Lord, discovering all that He has put in us to do and be. Looking for Him, seeking Him and His will, properly positions you to uncover His plan for your life. Are you looking for love? Start by sincerely looking for God. Adjust your focus to pursue Him and all that He has in store. He says to you,

> And ye shall seek Me, and find Me, when ye shall search for Me with all your heart. Jeremiah 29:13

I. MARRIAGE IS GOD'S IDEA

And the Lord God said, It is not good that the man should be alone; I will make an help meet for him. Genesis 2:18

"A FAULTY CONCEPT OF MARRIAGE LEADS TO ERRONEOUS EXPECT-ATIONS AND UNDULY PLACES A STRAIN ON THE PERSON THAT WANTS TO UNDERSTAND HOW TO LOVE YOU."

When listening to some of my all-time favorite songs, I try to surmise what the writer was thinking when the song was being constructed. What was the writer going through, what was their mood or inspiration? Although you can somewhat gather the answers to those questions as you interpret the song, it would add so much color to the picture in your mind if you knew first-hand what the songwriter was thinking. To fully understand something, it would be great to talk to the inventor of it to listen to their instructions. Just imagine how frustrating it would be trying to put together a complex item without a manual. Reading the manual makes it so much easier than trying to wing it and assembling something on the fly. Unfortunately, many approach marriages that way. To fully understand marriage, we need to seek wisdom from the mind of the Creator of marriage, which is God Himself. His Word is the manual for life and gives profound insight into marriage.

A faulty concept of marriage leads to erroneous expectations and unduly places a strain on the person that wants to understand how to love you. Love is about sacrificing for and focusing on the needs of your husband or wife. The goal is for this to be done reciprocally, which will make for an incredible life together. Some have given up on love. Past experiences of hurt and relationships that soured can dampen your hopes of ever being in a satisfying marriage. I always say,

IF YOU'VE GIVEN UP ON LOVE, YOU
HAVE GIVEN UP ON GOD BECAUSE

GOD IS LOVE (1 JOHN 4:8).

There are obstructions to finding love; most often, people get in their own way through unwise choices, misguided notions about love, and fairytale expectations. Love is more than an idea, and in too many relationships, people are in love with the idea of marriage instead of the person that they're involved with. All these thoughts need to be stripped away so that we can think with the right perspective to be able to have loving, fulfilling relationships.

Many have gone from "I do," to "I no longer want to." Having vowed before God Almighty and many witnesses to love, honor, and cherish, for better or worse, for richer or poorer, in sickness and in health until death, along the way, something or some things happened, and they no longer want to be with that person. They say, "we grew apart, my needs have changed, we couldn't get along, money trouble, concerns about the kids, unfaithfulness, lies, abuse," and the list goes on.

What God has given to the human family in marriage was designed to be a beautiful gift and a blessing, but unfortunately, because of an improper understanding of God's intent, it deteriorates to a place where great heartache and pain occurs. How do you define marriage? Have you ever really thought of the meaning? Marriage is often fantasized about, planned for, and then entered. But how many consider the spiritual nature of marriage?

For some, marriage is a very serious consideration. While for others, it is entered into recklessly. There are some that avoid marriage like the plague. They see marriage as a prison term, sentenced to life without fun, or something to be considered when they get much older. It's difficult for them to understand how anyone would want to spend the rest of their life with the same person. They would much rather get into relationships in a disconnected kind of way, no real commitment, or expectations.

There is a natural, physical component to marriage, but the primary aspect of marriage that isn't really considered is the spiritual one. Marriage should be first understood in a spiritual context because it was founded and ordained by God Himself. Therefore, it is critical to understand what God had in mind concerning marriage to have the kind of marriage that brings a lifetime of happiness and fulfillment. Marriage is not an invention of man or something that humanity has stumbled upon. For all the discoveries that humanity has made, marriage was not one of them. Marriage was birthed out of the mind of an all-wise God.

Marriage is typically defined as being the institution or consensual union between a man and a woman in a relationship to legally live together as husband and wife, but as we'll see through this writing, it is infinitely more than that. The subject of marriage has become a matter of great debate and controversy, as there is a push to redefine what marriage is. But what this writing will seek to do is to establish the biblical template of what marriage was intended to be. According to what God ordained, marriage is to be between a man and a woman.

Marriage is the deepest, most intimate relationship in the human experience. It differs from all other relationships in the sense that it is a process of a man and woman becoming one based on the promise to be faithful to one another. It is the experiencing of each other, spiritually, physically, and emotionally.

> Therefore, shall a man leave his father and
> mother, and shall cleave unto his wife: and
> they shall be one flesh (Genesis 2:24).

A man leaves his parents to cleave to his wife, thus forming a new family unit. And so, the process begins of the two becoming one. It is during the process of becoming one that can bring about difficulty and problems. How is it that two different individuals can become one? Two people who are unique and distinct endeavoring to unite faith, perspectives, ideas, goals, and so on. Easily you can see the potential for conflict and adversity. The differences in their physiology are as pieces of a puzzle that fit together and extend that family through children birthed from their union. Concerning the differences in the makeup between men and women, God designed them to compliment and balance the relationship. What he is as a man fills the void for what she is not, being a woman. And what she brings to the marriage as a woman uniquely contributes to their union what he can't because he's a man. In other words, God wires the man in such a way to bring to the marriage things that are exclusive to him; likewise, He puts those things in the woman that are inimitable or unique to her. But the failure to understand this dynamic causes conflict which often leads to discord and divorce.

The numbers as it relates to the divorce rate in the US are alarming to say the least. Researchers estimate that 41% of all first marriages end in divorce, not including those that are legally separated. Before we can understand some of the reasons; let's delve into the numbers a little deeper. While the divorce rate for first marriages is approaching 50%, second marriages have a divorce rate of about 60%, and third marriages have a divorce rate of around 73%.

There are also the many couples that are unhappy in their marriages, but for reasons like the sake of the kids, finances, to avoid embarrassment or to keep the house, they stay together. With the prevalence of marriages failing, many have lost interest in being married. This has caused an influx of people in relationships with unusual terms, undefined parameters, and unclear goals.

II. DESTINY DATING (POTENTIAL)

"FOR A DESTINY DATER, DATING IS THE RELATIONSHIP BETWEEN YOU AND SOMEONE, WHERE YOU EXERCISE PRAYERFUL CONSIDERATION ABOUT THE POTENTIAL OF WHAT THE TWO OF YOU COULD BE TOGETHER; BUT IT SHOULD NEVER BYPASS THE CORDIAL ACQUAINTANCE STAGE."

When you understand that you are a person of destiny and purpose, you view all of life with that perspective. You don't speak in terms of luck or chance; you don't see things as happening randomly or by coincidence; you believe that God is ordering your steps and overseeing the episodes of your life; you believe and trust that He will bring that person into your life that is meant for you. You're not picky, you're just purposeful. You understand the importance of not making decisions out of desperation and the need for wise discretion. For a destiny dater, dating is the relationship between you and someone, where you exercise prayerful consideration about the potential of what the two of you could be together; but it should never bypass the cordial acquaintance stage. Unfortunately, there's often a rush to romance that results in the sin of fornication and the couple merely mimicking the lifestyle of being married. When there's casual dating with no protective barriers or real intentions of getting married, it often leads to immorality. The rush to romance approach skips over the necessary friendship stage during which time the two can really get to know each other. When things are rushed, romance is presumed, sometimes even forced, but may not be the natural progression of your relationship. It is often the case that two people should only be friends, or brothers and sisters in the Lord. There are too many times that people attempt to be romantically involved with someone, and when it goes off the rails, it ends with the two not even being able to be friendly with each other or on speaking terms. The mindset should be friends first, and not the so-called friends with benefits mentality which is nothing more than sex partners attempting to avoid commitment. As a genuine friendship develops, that time is not wasted if it doesn't result in marriage. At a minimum, it will be the start of having a lifelong friend, or if it does develop romantically, it will serve to be a foundation for the relationship during times of adversity because they enjoy each other's company. Friendship provides an environment where love can be birthed.

I have seen many situations where people were in relationships simply to pass time, knowing that they weren't genuinely interested in being with that person in the long term. They see the relationship as "something to do" to prevent boredom, inadvertently leading that person on and setting them up for heartbreak. Even if you have made it clear where you stand, to continue in a relationship, giving false hope to someone that is developing feelings and getting attached is selfish and unfair.

It's important to think properly when considering a relationship. If at the beginning it is established that the two will only have friendly interaction and honor the Lord in how they relate to one another, this will go a long way in protecting them from doing things that are not pleasing to God. This brings us to another important point, which is the need to be with a person that is like-minded and wants to live a God-glorifying life. The Word of the Lord tells us to,

> not be unequally yoked together with unbelievers: for what fellowship has righteousness with unrighteousness? And what communion has light with darkness? (2 Cor.

6:14).

A person that has experienced God's saving grace and is living to do His will is going contrary to God's counsel when they pursue someone that is not likeminded.

When a believer, living for the Lord, gets involved with an unsaved person, they usually do it with the intentions of helping that person to get saved. Many times, what happens is the unsaved person pulls the saved person away from their focus on the things of God and compromising takes place. The saved person and the unsaved individual have things "in common," albeit, the worse things; they both have the sin nature. That commonality is what often causes them to get involved in sinful things that are offensive to God. The unsaved person is living through that sin nature and may influence the saved person to behaviors that God has called them out of.

Determining who to spend time with should be approached with prayerful contemplation. If you are a believer in the Lord, seeking to live for Him, it would be wise to not use worldly criteria to decide who is worth your time and effort. Let's unpack that thought. Instead of prioritizing things that are superficial, at the top of your checklist should be substantive things like: Are they a person of godly character? Do they exhibit faith and kindness? And are they in pursuit of God's will for their life? These are the types of things that should also define the caliber of the person you are and what you find to be attractive and beautiful when you see it in someone.

Finding "the one" is more about finding yourself and God's purpose for your life (destiny). The one that He has for you will fit into your destiny because you will have that in common with the person. As you both are in pursuit of that "shared destiny," you'll realize it will take God's grace and the two of you helping each other to arrive at it. Destiny dating includes mutually growing in God and discovering how your gifts are cohesive and blend together. It is important to understand the calling of God that is on your life, the gifts, and abilities that God has given us to be impactful in service to Him, and where He wants to take us as we grow and mature in our Christian journey.

Don't let your decision to begin a relationship be out of loneliness, frustration, or to help to distance yourself from past relationships. Let it be from your prayerfulness, pursuit of purpose, and desire to fulfill your destiny. Seek God to become whole and content, satisfied and at peace by yourself, so that you don't place a burden on someone to come into your life to make you happy. That would make the relationship be about you, promoting selfishness and creating resentment; that's destructive dating. Destiny dating is about the potential and wonderful possibilities that God allows you to see in someone, and how the attributes of you and that person will configure to fulfill God's purpose in bringing you together.

III. A CRACKED MIRROR

"A MIRROR THAT IS DAMAGED OR CRACKED WILL REFLECT A DISTORTED PICTURE OF THE TRUTH."

Dating can be a time of false representations and pretense. Much like the way that people post their best pictures on social media, showing their happiest times; dating is when many create a version of themselves that is disingenuous and fake. This charade continues over time with effort and energy that should be used to cultivate and build a true friendship based on the reality of who you both are. Time shouldn't be wasted pretending and trying to impress. We are all people with issues, faults, and failures. An unfortunate fact is that during the time of being single, people chafe away, longing to be with someone. Being single should be about "being better," optimizing that time to advance in every area of your life, which will produce benefits for you while you're single and if you get married. Formulate a plan and execute it; examine your issues, and work to get them resolved. Improve your finances by attacking debt, clean out the clutter from your past, focus on your health. Excel in your career, expand your education, and most importantly, draw closer to the Lord by prioritizing Him in your life, which is plenty to occupy your attention and drive you to a flourishing future.

It's important to be honest with yourself and to make an accurate assessment of your issues. This is not always easy to do as we may give ourselves the benefit of the doubt, always seeing ourselves as being justified in our actions or as the innocent victim. Self-evaluations can be a tall order, and we may fall short of giving the correct analysis of ourselves, especially if our viewpoint is tainted because of what I call a "cracked mirror perception." It would be a rare thing for any of us to leave the house without, at some point, looking at ourselves in the mirror. When we first rise from sleep, it's not long before we glance at ourselves in the mirror. When we peer into the mirror, we want to see what others will see when they look at us; we want to be sure that we're presenting our best appearance.

A mirror that is damaged or cracked will reflect a distorted picture of the truth. It will tell you that you are broken, split, or fragmented into pieces. It will make you look larger in some places or smaller in others. A cracked mirror is a source of lies. Just like a cracked mirror, many see themselves through a lying lens or from a polluted opinion that reflects low self-worth and drags them down into living a life of settling and accepting less than what they desire. For others, this faulty perspective causes them to have an inflated mindset about who they are, and they look down their nose at everyone. The truth of who we are is revealed in God's Word. When we investigate the Word, we see our need for God and His salvation through Jesus Christ. We are tainted by the sin nature in need of God's grace. Our fallen humanity is the culprit that causes friction in our relationships and brings challenges in life.

Our estimation of ourselves is therefore rooted in sin. We need the light of God's Word to shine on us to expose and lay us bare. When God makes us understand who we are, why we are, and all the issues and matters that pertain to us; it's incumbent upon us to commit ourselves to His care for healing and deliverance. When two people that are broken, are sin-tainted, and have a faulty mentality come together attempting to begin a relationship, they will travel on rough terrain trying to navigate their way through issues that stem from having a cracked mirror perception.

A necessary step that leads to being in a relationship that will be fulfilling and built to last is in having the right acuity of yourself and your eagerness to carry your concerns to God. You need to know your weaknesses, vulnerabilities, and reasons for why you're prone to doing the things that you do. Many don't want to take that trip inward and aren't prepared to confront the ugliness that may be uncovered, and many simply don't know how to go about digging into their own heart to unearth what hides in the depths of their being. That inability or unwillingness to allow God's Word to probe through the halls of your heart leaves you with a defective mentality that will only impair your relationships.

This explains why so many continue in relationships with people that obviously mean them no good or are abusive. Their mindset has great difficulty discerning when they are being mistreated like a person with crippled legs may struggle to walk. A cracked mirror perception is dangerous, in that it accepts harmful behavior and normalizes it. Sadly, this type of mindset can become a deep-seated, generational mentality as children grow up witnessing a parent that limps from a bad relationship to worse.

People with this mentality usually become desensitized from what's good for them. They may even struggle with being treated right; having developed a callous, indifferent attitude from the time they endured ugly treatment in past relationships.

Only God's Word can renew your mind and deliver you from this deadly mentality, revealing to you your true worth and significance. If this cracked mirror perspective has been your frame of thinking, understand that the Father loves you and has set His heart upon you. No matter what your life has been, in Christ, you can begin again with His promises nestled in your heart, knowing that He has in mind for you "plans to prosper you and not to harm you, plans to give you hope and a future", Jeremiah 29:11 (NIV).

SECTION 2: LEARNING

Learning

Employers typically prefer to hire the person that has experience in the position that's vacant. There are many things for the new hire to learn, so when that person comes with experience, it saves time. That previous experience will help the new hire to settle in the job, being familiar with what needs to be done, which gives the employer confidence that they know how to do it. Knowledge and skill can be acquired by doing a particular thing. Going through, enduring, and being a part of something, gives you experience in it. The critical thing, however, is to be able to extract the lessons from it.

We all make mistakes, through bad choices, and poor decision making. Too often, our own experiences provide lessons that we ignore. There are hurts and wounds that could have been avoided had we simply learned from the past. An important question to ask yourself is, "what do the choices and decisions I've made say about me and who I am?" Before we can be in a fulfilling relationship, we will need to first understand ourselves; our weaknesses, strengths, proclivities, needs etc.

As we delve into a discussion about relationships and how we can discover and experience the sweetness of love, I want to interject a crucial point. The most important relationship that anyone of us could ever have is the one that we must have with our Creator. As we draw closer to the Lord, sincerely submitting ourselves to His providence, the better positioned we'll be to give ourselves in a loving relationship where there's honesty and transparency. The learning curve is a life-long process of gaining knowledge about yourself, as well as the one you love, and most importantly, God Himself. In *2 Peter 3:18*, we're told, "But grow in grace, and in the knowledge of our Lord and savior Jesus Christ."

IV. GUARDED

Keep thy heart with all diligence; for out of it are the issues of life. Proverbs 4:23

"IT TAKES TIME TO TRUST A PERSON AND TO ALLOW THEM TO SEE THE INNER WORKINGS OF OUR HEART."

You may be hurting, feeling like you're losing at life and losing at love. Through frayed relationships or maybe a divorce, you're left with a wounded, leaking heart. The conversation about relationships and marriage is depressing to you because you feel like you've lost so much and have been drained of what used to be hopeful expectations. Some are in dating situations or may be in a marriage, but they are struggling with a darkened outlook on love. Gone are the smiles, the laughter, and the excitement. You feel like an empty shell, wishing that you had more to offer. You feel like you've given so much in the past and haven't received back what you put out, and now, you're simply depleted. As you exit one relationship, you reluctantly go to the next, closed and shut down.

There's something that those types of people do that is unfair to their own prospects and the person that is interested in them. They view that person through the lens of where they've been. We often make our past relationships the point of reference and compare the new with the old. Of course, it's natural to measure things based on our experiences, but a conscious decision should be made that this person will have an opportunity to create on a blank canvas. We read in Proverbs 4:23, "Keep thy heart with all diligence; for out of it are the issues of life".

It takes time to trust a person and to allow them to see the inner workings of our heart. We guard our hearts because of past hurts, attempting to shield ourselves from any potential pain or disappointment. This often prevents you from experiencing the kind of relationship that your heart yearns for. The fear of being hurt hinders your ability to trust, and those protective measures can cause frustration to the person that is honestly interested in loving and caring for you—pushing them away. How do we go about opening ourselves up and at the same time protecting ourselves from being let down? The key is in being better equipped to make wise choices while also understanding that a world that is pain-free doesn't exist. There will be hurts and disappointments even when you finally get together with the one that is an answer to all your prayers.

We also should be mindful that we will have our times of being the one that causes pain and disappointment. When you have offended or injured someone, how are you at asking for forgiveness, seeking to repair and restore? Are you humble and conciliatory? Or do you refuse to admit your wrongs? Thinking that we can escape experiencing these types of things is an unrealistic expectation. So, there is a balance that needs to be struck between carefully, prayerfully observing possible relationships, while at the same time acknowledging our own imperfections. The openness that makes marriage beautiful requires that we remove the barriers that we hide behind attempting to keep our heart safe. The main thing to remember is that a closed, guarded heart doesn't make for a beautiful marriage; it only places a wedge between two hearts that are meant to blend into one.

As it relates to your relationship, you may be somewhat successful at protecting your heart, but what have you really accomplished when it comes to advancing a loving, trusting environment? The answer is nothing. So, for the heart that has been wounded, guarding it doesn't bring you closer to a mutually satisfying relationship; it only makes you feel secure. The thing that causes relationships to blossom is the steady acquisition of trust and constantly fighting to close off your heart works against that. When you exercise wise discretion and begin to allow your heart to be exposed to someone that you perceive to be trustworthy, and they validate that decision, trust is cultivated. The more your heart is convinced that it is safe, the more you open and disclose the inner tick tocks of your being. This process of the two of you gradually exposing pieces and portions of your heart is what knits you together.

Sometimes, people with similar scars are attracted to each other, mistaking their commonalities for being reasons to be together. They find a sense of relief in sharing their history of hurts, and the lines get blurred between romance and reason. In these types of relationships, the couple's focus is on bleeding together and venting about how they've been injured over the years, never allowing their wounds to heal. A bond may be formed, but not necessarily a healthy one. The ability to jointly air grievances doesn't mean that you should be a couple; it may simply mean that you've found someone that you're comfortable sharing those grievances with. This is like the AA/NA experience, where a group comes together to share their struggles and experiences with substance abuse. When it comes to finding a place to park your heart for the rest of your life, you want to hand over the keys to someone that won't only relate to your pain but will join you on your journey to wholeness and love.

The priority for people with wounded hearts should be healing. The heart that is hurting and guarded will struggle to love properly because its focus is on protecting itself. You want to be loved and to give love; but before you can really be in a loving relationship where heart communes with heart, give it to God to guard. As it relates to couples, guardedness is in opposition to intimacy. Intimacy is the conversation between two hearts: it's the hearts of lovers singing, in harmony, a melody of love unheard by ears. To experience that type of depth in your marriage, God brings about healing, closing the gashes. The past will leave scars; but they will serve as lessons and reminders. You can learn from where you've been, being better prepared to see danger without ignoring the signs. Your past can be turned into a positive in that you now realize what you don't want. Don't allow the hurtful things from your yesterday to extinguish the love in your heart that you want to give. Your heart is safe with God; trust Him to protect it.

V. WAVELENGTHS

"ANGER IS OFTEN COMMUNICATED
EVEN WITHOUT WORDS BEING
SPOKEN. IT IS A THICK PRESENCE
THAT YELLS LOUDLY THROUGH
THE TIGHTLY CLOSED LIPS OF A
PERSON THAT IS FURIOUS"

We all should know the importance of communication when it comes to relationships and how the undoing of marriages is often traced back to the couple's inability to communicate. A major part of communication that we may not think about is listening. It's not just about getting your point across, but it is necessary to listen, which helps us to understand. When there's a disagreement or dispute between you and your spouse, what will help to diffuse the tension is viewing it through the right perspective. In the grand scheme of things, the dispute poses a threat to there being peace and joy in your home, and nothing should be allowed to compromise that. The things that should be communicated through what we say, even during our disputes, is our desire to maintain love and peace in our home ... along with our willingness to hear the other side of the argument, and the ability to admit when we are wrong.

Anger is often communicated even without words being spoken. It is a thick presence that yells loudly through the tightly closed lips of a person that is furious. God's Word gives us wise counsel to help our anger to abate. James 1:19 says,

> Wherefore, my beloved brethren, let every man be swift to hear, slow to speak, slow to wrath: for the wrath of man worketh not the righteousness of God.

Interestingly, we naturally do the opposite of what God's Word tells us to do. We are slow to hear, fast to speak, and fast to wrath. Let's commit to being better listeners, hearing, even feeling, what's being communicated behind words spoken and learn to interpret their silence. Communication alone is not enough; what's needed is healthy communication that leads to comprehension, which encourages commitment.

It may be difficult for many in this generation to imagine that the type of programming that is watched on our smart TVs and devices today was listened to from around the 1920s to the 1950s. It was called the "golden age of radio." Families gathered around the radio to listen to play by play sports, variety shows, mysteries, soap operas, talent shows, westerns, and more. Radio technology is the communication of electromagnetic signals or waves being transmitted and identified. To hear your desired program, you locate it on the dial, knowing the time that it "airs." This transmission of signals and waves is very similar to what needs to happen for effective communication in our relationships. When there is anger, resentment, suspicion, and a refusal to forgive, these attitudes and feelings are transmitted through our words and actions. They become the static that fills relationships with interference and hinders couples from being able to communicate on a loving, pleasant level. The enemy of our soul would love nothing more than to project through us bad, weird vibes that gum up the flow of love between couples.

When it comes to conversations and the ability to communicate in our relationships, we need to be on the same wavelength to really understand each other. For some, talking is their least favorite thing to do when it comes to expressing feelings and sharing emotionally. They choose to avoid confrontation at all cost. To them, it's easier to stay in silence or to text and communicate on their gadgets and devices. Interestingly, communicating on social media, or our smart devices, as convenient as that is, makes us less social. We can simply text an Emoji that has the expression that we want to communicate without even experiencing that emotion. We can respond in a text with an LOL without even laughing out loud. All these things allow us to not have to face conflict in our relationships; we can hide behind a keyboard, laptop, or device and have the correspondence that should be face to face. When the inevitable happens, and you're face to face, it's awkward and empty. In many ways our devices are depriving us of real human interaction and are often the reason for misunderstandings and confusion. Things like body language, facial expressions, and the spirit that our presence emits is lost when there's no person-to-person engagement.

Isn't it interesting that a couple can speak the same language, but struggle trying to understand each other? It can be as if they are speaking in different languages. It's often the case that a person's silence is saying a lot. There are ways of getting on the same wavelength that will help us on our journey of love and discovery.

One of the most important things that lead to the meshing of two hearts is trust. When you realize that your heart is safe with that person, you have a comfort level that allows you to express freely the innermost thoughts of your heart. There are signals and vibrations that we give off and being transparent and genuine builds a trusting platform on which true communication can be achieved.

Concerning marriage, husbands are encouraged in the Word to "dwell (be physically present) with your wife according to knowledge" (1 Peter 3:7).

* * *

Knowledge is acquired through study, experience, and revelation. That means, pay attention to your wife by being sensitive to her needs, notice what channel she's on, her moods, and the best times to discuss any concerns or issues. Learn how to decode her unspoken signals. Likewise, the wife is to observe her husband and patiently allow him to find how to articulate his heart. Prayerfully seek wisdom to be able to decipher his gestures and actions. As you grow together, you become connected in the Spirit, and will be able to sense things in each other without it being said, because you're on the same wavelength.

VI. MORE THAN SKIN

"FORNICATION IS THE COUNTER-FEIT OF MARRIAGE."

The sexuality of mankind was given by God to be a tremendous blessing, not just for procreation, but to strengthen the marital bond and for the enjoyment of intimacy. Sexual relations should be about more than just skin on skin and bodies in motion. Although sex between husband and wife is a physical interaction, it is intended by God to be a pathway into a spiritual sphere where hearts communicate and are reassured of faithful commitment. The sexual inclination or desire is a natural part of our human makeup, albeit a strong part. But in that it's only a portion of us, it should not consume us. God didn't intend for us to lust for sex, never considering the consequences of our choices. Lust is an appetite for sex that is out of control; it is more than what is normal. With human sexuality being a natural part of us, there are those that have seized upon that opportunity to profit from selling sexually explicit material.

The porn industry has been a booming business for many years, as it appeals to the sin nature that dwells in all of us. Porn is presented in a false package with performers that often are surgically enhanced and give the impression that they are enjoying the brutality and disrespect that they are experiencing in the films. With the arrival of the internet, many of the porn shops and adult video stores have had to close because of easy access and free content available online. Some of the actresses feel that they must resort to doing riskier, degrading, sexual stunts to demand more money to offset their losses because of the free material that's available.

What a perversion of the intention of God and what He designed sex to be within the beautiful bonds of marriage. But herein hides the deception; for it is thought that marriage constricts and limits one's freedom to explore human sexuality, when in fact, the opposite is true. While it is true that marriage has boundaries that God in His wisdom has established to protect and bless us, it is also true that within the parameters that He has set, we are free to give fully and completely all of ourselves to the person that we have pledged to faithfully love for a lifetime. This exploration and journey into the vast possibilities of love are limitless between a man and his wife that has God's blessings upon their union.

It's important to emphasize the point that sexual desire is a God-given, normal tendency. It should be differentiated, however, from lust. The God-given sexual desire was designed to find its release within the union of marriage. It is not to be released through the perversion of fornication (sex between unmarried people). Fornication is the counterfeit of marriage. It is sinful behavior in the eyes of God, and it is dishonoring to the people involved. The Greek word for fornication, as it appears in the New Testament, is "pornea," from where the word pornography is partly derived. It describes all sexual activity that violates God's purpose, function, and intention. Fornication is a general umbrella term that a lot of today's sexual conduct fits under.

Lust is the perversion of what God intended

for us, which is love, properly expressed in marriage.

> Marriage should be honored by all, and the marriage bed kept pure, for God will judge the adulterer and all the sexually immoral, Hebrews 13:4 NIV.

Lust is everything that God doesn't want for us; it is uncontrolled and unleashed sexual desire like a fire burning on the outside of a fireplace. Lust leads to fornication; the sexual activity that doesn't coincide or agree with God's ordained purpose.

The apostle Paul in writing to believers at Corinth (which was an idolatrous, immoral city in New Testament times) gives us understanding concerning the problem of fornication. In 1 Corinthians 6:13 he says,

> Meats for the belly, and the belly for meats: but God shall destroy both it and them. Now the body is not for fornication, but for the Lord, and the Lord for the body.

The point being that we naturally have an appetite, so we eat food, but the body (that naturally has a desire for sex) we are to surrender to the Lord and His design for sexual expression. For the One that created and designed the human body knows what's best for it.

Some simply indulge their sexual impulses whenever they arise with whoever they wish (fornication). They are only concerned about themselves and relieving their sexual urges. The one that they lust for is nothing more than an object to please them. This is the product that pornography sells; it promises to satisfy your lustful fantasies, and sexual cravings. The performers understand that their objective is to be desirable, accommodating, and willing to do whatever it takes to produce sexually arousing material; no matter how humiliating the scene, their job is to be convincing that this is what they want.

All of this takes a devastating toll upon those that view and absorb this type of content (video and pictures), and certainly upon those that participate in it. In ministry, we often encounter people that have been grossly and negatively impacted by pornography. It shows up predominately in the way that men view women, and even in the way those men and women view themselves. Women are of course objectified, and men are dehumanized. While women in this material are reduced to being nothing more than toys to please, men are portrayed as barbaric, uncaring savages. And the sad but unfortunate reality is that many people endeavor to bring the lies of pornography into their relationships and marriages only to get destructive results.

In the marital union, a husband and wife are to be knitted together into a fabric of committed love. Their commitment to each other, through Christ, is intricately and delicately woven over time to be a seamless, strong material. But that fabric is threatened to be ripped and torn when porn and other false representations of sexuality are brought into the marriage.

Those that defend pornography contend that viewing the material brings excitement and passion to their marriage, but the truth is that they have introduced devastation and poisonous venom into their relationship, and the false intimacy that pornography presents will mutilate the marriage. Often, the porn viewer will become detached and disconnected from his or her spouse, preferring the ease of a fantasy relationship. The brain having been so inundated with perverted pleasure; the porn viewer can't appreciate appropriate pleasure. Pornography reduces human love relationships to the level of animalistic impulses. It puts all the emphasis on the sexual and physical but ignores, even eliminates the spiritual, relational, and emotional aspect of our being. Unfortunately, our times reflect a graphic, loose, unrestrained attitude from the way that people dress to the shameless conversations that they engage in. That lascivious, brazen behavior is consuming our society like a cancer.

Relationships suffer many times because couple's often struggle with communication and being able to express their emotions and feelings to each other. When someone gives themselves away sexually in marriage, it is meant to be the ultimate way of saying "I love you and I'm faithfully committed to you"; that's the way that God, in His infinite wisdom, has designed it. But having sex has deteriorated to the same level as that of a casual handshake or high five. People think nothing more of having sex than just a random experience with no consideration, emotional investment, or commitment. Pornography is encouraging and causing this type of mentality to permeate throughout our society.

There is a healthy openness that should exist between a husband and his wife. It is the kind of openness where they can freely express their hopes and dreams and even their fears to each other and feel safe in doing so. There is a misconception when it comes to intimacy where it is understood to be primarily physical or sexual, but that's merely a portion of the whole. Real intimacy is beyond a husband and wife coming together sexually; it is the full and complete revealing of ourselves to the one that we have vowed to love for as long as we live. It is the steady unveiling of the inner you to your spouse. It is so much more than your husband or wife seeing your physical nakedness; it is purposely exhibiting your internal nakedness and walking your spouse into the essence of your heart. Without any pretense or deceit, intimacy is when you're able to just be who you truly are in front of your spouse.

Opposite of that, pornography encourages random sex between the unmarried, those that aren't your spouse, and even between strangers. It is an attack on truth, perverting and distorting the real picture of what marriage, love, and sex should look like. That attack has left many people, even the young that buy the lies, destroyed, and families torn apart. But God is a healer and not just of sick bodies; He also can heal a warped mind that has been a dumping ground for the misrepresentations of pornography. God wants to heal marriages and resurrect relationships that seem to have expired. He wants to purge out the images of pornography that have been embedded in the minds of many.

An entire generation of young people is being exposed to pornography and their mind is being polluted against the institution of marriage. Virgins are relentlessly teased and pressured to have sex by their peers and encouraged to give in by the entertainment industry and media. And sadly, the church, at large, because of compromising and a trending away from the standard of God, isn't a steadfast example for them to witness the right way. The right way is to develop an appreciation for the intangibles, the inner qualities that outlast physical features and to look for those character traits a person possesses that will impact your heart.

SECTION 3: LOVING

Loving

In football games, the place kicker has the job of kick-offs, kicking a three-point field goal and kicking for the extra point after a touchdown. I remember many times watching football games and seeing the players line up for the kick; and when the camera was set showing the goal posts, you would sometimes see a fan in the stands, holding a sign that said, St. John 3:16. To those of us that are familiar with the Bible, we know that verse to be one of the more known scriptures in the Word of God. It reads,

> For God so loved the world, that He gave His only begotten Son, that whosoever believeth in Him should not perish, but have everlasting life.

Consider the difference the word "so" makes in that verse. If it read, For God loved the world and gave His only begotten son; that would be saying plenty. But with it saying that He "so loved the world", that pulls back the curtain between time and eternity, and let's us glimpse into the heart of God. Just how much is "so" much? What exactly are we to think of God "so" loving us?

As an adverb, so means "to such a degree or to a

great extent." It's such a small word but helps us to emphasize the amount of something and leaves open ended how much it can be. God's love for us is expansive and eternal. We don't have the vocabulary to sum up all that God is, but He is in a word, "love".

Loving your spouse should be <u>dimensional and intentional</u>. Dimensional, because in expressing your love, you will break through barriers and resistance, expanding to new levels and degrees. Intentional, because we consciously give our love on purpose. Beyond the physical and displaying a love that is spiritual. Through the peaceful and stormy times of life, we grow in our capacity to love, without conditions or limits, modelling love to look like the love of the Savior. In this third section of the book, we will look at some of the things that come to test the depth of our love in marriage, and how being rooted and grounded in God anchors us on an unmovable foundation.

> That Christ may dwell in your hearts by faith; that ye, being rooted and grounded in love, may be able to comprehend with all saints what is the breadth, and length, and depth, and height; and to know the love of Christ, which passeth knowledge, that ye might be filled with all the fulness of God. Ephesians 3:17-19

VII. YOUR MARRIAGE IS YOUR MINISTRY

**"IN MARRIAGE, THE RELINQUISH-
ING OF SELF-CENTEREDNESS AND
THE DISCARDING OF A PERSONAL
AGENDA, SETS THE STAGE FOR
GIVING AND SACRIFICE."**

Consider the people that we call great, actors, singers, musicians, athletes, the rich, and the famous. We marvel at their abilities, skills, and their talent. They are held in high esteem and praised for the way that they entertain us, their creativity, and giftedness. But the Word of the Lord defines greatness in a drastically different way. The Lord teaches us what true greatness is in St. Matthew 20:20–28. In the account, we read of the request from the mother of James and John to Christ, "Grant that these, my two sons, may sit, the one on thy right hand, and the other on the left, in thy kingdom."

In His response to her, He goes on to say that the leaders of this world that are "called great" exercise dominion and authority over the people. Then comes the powerful truth in verses 26–28:

> But it shall not be so among you: but whosoever will be great among you, let him be your minister; And whosoever will be chief among you, let him be your servant: Even as the Son of man came not to be ministered unto, but to minister, and to give his life a ransom for many.

Christ Himself, who is the greatest of all, God in the flesh, came to minister (serve). The very One that all human history will bow to and honor as King of kings and Lord of lords, served. The word ministry means service; to minister is to serve. A "minister" is more than someone with a title; it is a calling. Ministers serve the people by attending to their needs.

In marriage, the concept is amplified. It's all about having a mindset to serve your spouse. Premarital counseling should prepare couples and advise them of the need to adopt this way of thinking. An unfortunate mistake by many leaders in the church has been the failure to make the point that candidates for marriage need the frame of mind to mutually serve one another. What makes for a beautiful marriage is being thoughtful, considerate, and selfless when it comes to your spouse. And demonstrating a willingness to put the needs of your spouse before your own is vital. We should seek to find ways in which we can assist our spouse in becoming all that God has ordained for them to be. This exposes the need to be close to Christ and to have a genuine relationship with Him as Savior and Lord. Being close to the Lord will motivate you to pray for your spouse, encourage your spouse and love your spouse. When we think of ministry, things like preaching, teaching and outreach to the homeless and inmates, and overseas missions comes to mind. But what should also come to mind is marriage. Marriage is ministry, and ministry necessitates prayerfulness, preparation, patience, planning, and power.

In all our human relationships, only marriage is designed by God to illustrate His eternal love for the church. In marriage, the relinquishing of self-centeredness and the discarding of a personal agenda, sets the stage for giving and sacrifice. This does not mean that you are forsaking who you are or that you are to lose yourself in the pursuit of pleasing your spouse, but it is the discovery and realization of who the two of you are together. It's no longer "you," it's now "the two of you" becoming one. Your spouse should benefit and be blessed by the presence of God in your life. In your marriage, you are an avenue through which God wants your spouse to experience and feel His love in a tangible way. God literally wants to work through you to impact your spouse. There are needs that are legitimate, and then there are perceived needs that are merely spurious or artificial. It is the legitimate needs that we endeavor to identify and meet as a spouse. Through communication and relationship, we learn and discover the needs of our spouse.

At this point, I want to stress the importance of being true and transparent. Too often, people mask themselves trying to hide their issues and insecurities. This is a dangerous game to play because what happens is people get married having successfully hidden the deep needs that are in them. The marriage takes place, and over time, a comfort level sets in, which is when the real you becomes evident. And people are left feeling that they were lied to and deceived when those ugly issues manifest; thus, creating trust issues and resentment.

To present a so-called you, that is not really you, is to "embody an illusion." When this is the case, the marriage will face unnecessary difficulties and struggles. By not allowing yourself to be the person that you are, you are in effect denying yourself true love, because true love is based on someone loving you as you are. This is how God loves us and why we don't deny the issues and needs that we have, but we acknowledge and surrender them to Him. The Lord didn't wait until we turned our lives around before He loved us; if that were the case, He would still be waiting. But the Word of the Lord says in Romans 5:7-8 NIV:

> Very rarely will anyone die for a righteous man, though for a good man someone might possibly dare to die. But God demonstrates his own love for us in this: While we were still sinners, Christ died for us.

Have we ever considered that the Lord, Jesus Christ, our Savior wants to work through us to meet the needs of our spouse? God wants vessels that He can use for His glory; instruments through which He can work. And it's through marriage where His love is to be expressed and demonstrated in an intimate way. The process of becoming one becomes more fluid when you understand what your spouse needs. This in no way is to suggest that my job is to fix my wife or that I'm a project for her to work on. The point is to love them with the love of Christ and to be instrumental in their edification and growth. At this point, it should be more and more apparent how much we need the One that ordained marriage to give us wisdom and insight as to how we can be a continuous blessing to our spouse. The overarching goal between a husband and wife is to assist one another in being everything that they are called of God to be. Not to be a hindrance or stumbling block but to encourage your spouse to reach their full potential in marriage, parenthood, their career, and every aspect of their being.

What's interesting in the Genesis account of the first man and woman is her place of origination. When God made the man, He made him of the dust of the ground and breathed into his nostrils the breath of life (Gen. 2:7). As for the woman, just as God scooped up clay and formed the man, He certainly could have done the same for her. But instead, He causes a deep sleep to come over the man and then extracts a rib, and from the rib of Adam, God makes Eve. From this we see several things; namely, the closeness, even oneness that God intends for a man and his wife; she is literally a part of him. The apostle Paul helps us to understand this truth in Ephesians 5 where he's giving instructions to husbands and wives, writing;

> As Christ loved the church, so ought men to love their wives (as their own bodies). He that loves his wife loves himself. For no man ever yet hated his own flesh; but nourishes and cherishes it, even as the Lord does the church. Ephesians 5:28-29.

A man that abuses his spouse in any form is

the equivalent of that same man injuring himself. Any man that would hold back his wife or is jealous and threatened by her success doesn't understand the goal of oneness and unity for marriage. By diminishing her, he's only succeeding at defeating and reducing himself. There is a false notion that "getting a woman is like a conquest." Sadly, that way of thinking carries into marriages, where men feel that their wives are to be conquered instead of cherished; what a tragic, unfortunate lie. She is not to be conquered; she's to be won, that is, convinced of his commitment and love for her. His life of obedience to God, his diligence, and his integrity causes his wife to have a heart that wraps around their home like a vine (see Psalm 128:3). Like the vine sticks to a house, she will attach herself to her home and family with a relentless love. Also like the vine, her love will expand and grow. This is a ministry of love between husband and wife; actively loving one another in such a way to inspire more love from each other.

VIII. ANNIVERSARIES AND ADVERSITY

"NOT ONLY DO WE MUTUALLY DISCOVER THINGS ABOUT EACH OTHER IN MARRIAGE, BUT YOU DISCOVER THINGS ABOUT YOUR-SELF AS TESTS AND TRIALS EXPOSE OUR STRENGTHS AND WEAK-NESSES."

L ove is to be enjoyed and celebrated throughout your marriage. During the time that you are together, you experience many things, some of which are difficult and test the depth of your commitment to each other. Special times, occasions and events are noted within your relationship. Whether it is the first time that you went out, the day you got engaged, or your wedding anniversary, these special dates remind us of when it all began, and we reflect on them and celebrate the fact that time has not eroded the love that we have for each other.

Some, however, even though they're still together, aren't necessarily happy. Adversity is a part of life and often exposes areas in our lives where we're weak and in need of strengthening. Marriages face fidelity issues, sickness, financial struggles, parental concerns, and other types of challenges. These things test our faith in God and our love for each other. There are couples that would say that the adversity they've faced together has dampened what used to be a passionate, loving relationship. The suddenness of adversity can flip our world upside down and leave us scrambling to regain our composure. In 2012, when I was diagnosed with cancer, it completely caught my wife and me by surprise. We just recently had our first daughter and were awaiting the arrival of our second that very month. I discovered, through that ordeal, how trials can push you into a greater seeking of God, make you more keenly aware of your mortality, and cause you to appreciate love with a deeper understanding.

In our marriages, there will be mountain top experiences as well as valley experiences. I have come to a place where I can sincerely thank God for having gone through cancer, the treatments, the tears, and the triumph of seeing the Lord completely heal me. During that difficult time of physical sickness and mental anguish, I began to understand more deeply the brevity of life, the beauty of life, the blessing of life, and that spending time with your family is a treasure from God.

Adversity can also bring out the worst in us and drive a wedge between husband and wife. It can draw out your selfishness, where you're only considering yourself, narrowly focusing on how you feel. We should see adversity through the eyes of faith, understanding that a loving God won't allow us to be tested beyond what we can handle (see 1 Cor. 10:13). As preachers, we often refer to the book of Job that deals with tremendous suffering and the loss that Job experienced. In looking at the account of how he suffered the loss of his great wealth, the tragic loss of his ten children, and the loss of his health, we don't give much attention to the fact that his wife was also devastated. In that they were married, his trouble was her trouble, and his loss was her loss. In a marriage, what one goes through has an impact on both, because you're one. It was coming to terms with the loss of her children and having to care for her sick husband that would cause her to become Satan's mouthpiece as she said to Job, "do you still retain your integrity? Curse God and die." (Job 2:9).

Obviously, she was at the end of her rope and spoke out of her great hurt and despair. When couples are dealing with adverse circumstances, they should be extra careful in how they talk to each other. During times of pressure, it becomes much easier to speak harshly and to be short tempered. The smallest thing can trigger you into a rage, causing a fiery blowup where things are said that can be difficult to forget and get past.

It's so important to be mindful that what you go through impacts your spouse, and not just see your angle. In dealing with cancer, it would have been easy for me to be wrapped up in my own concerns about my health and future, but I also had to be concerned about my pregnant wife and what were her worries. Is her faith wavering, is she fearful, is she hopeful? The day that I was initially scheduled for surgery had to be changed because it was the same day that my wife was to be induced into labor. Facing that adversity with my wife reminds me of a line from one of my favorite love songs by Anita Baker, Caught Up in the Rapture which says, "We stand side by side, till the storms of life pass us by." Every time I hear those lyrics from the song, it makes me think of devoted couples weathering fierce storms, standing shoulder to shoulder, upholding each other until the sun pierces through and the gloomy clouds lift, and together, they victoriously emerge from the debris with an even stronger faith in God and greater love for each other.

There may be times when one's faith is strong, and their spouse may have a faltering faith. That is not the time to denigrate them; it's the very time that love is needed. That's the time for them to see in you a love that won't let them go and assures them of your commitment. The fires of life should reveal our unwavering love for God and each other. That type of love will help to revive a spouse that is stumbling in life and produce in them a resolve to stand. Adversity reveals our character and inner fortitude, or the lack of it. Being in love means that we love even the not so favorable parts about our spouse. As ugly things become evident to us about our spouse, they become a part of our conversation, not criticism. Not only do we mutually discover things about each other in marriage, but you discover things about yourself as tests and trials expose our strengths and weaknesses. It's up to us to be honest with God, ourselves and then our spouse.

IX. INTIMATE EXPRESSIONS

"WE ARE SEXUAL BEINGS WITH URGES AND YEARNINGS FOR SEXUAL GRATIFICATION AND SHOULD UNDERSTAND THAT GOD HAS ORDAINED MARRIAGE AS THE OUTLET FOR THOSE DESIRES TO BE EXPRESSED AND FULFILLED."

A look on a person's face often tells the story of what that individual is going through; what we feel inwardly usually surfaces outwardly. Whether we are afraid, worried, happy, or mad, a facial expression can be the evidence of how we feel. Although some are good at maintaining a straight face or concealing their inner emotions, for the most part, we wear on our faces how we feel. We wear frowns that show when we are upset and smiles when we are happy and content

Love is meant to be demonstrated and shown in meaningful ways. When love is on display, it's never a question of "What is that?" Love is seen; love is heard; love is felt and easily identified. Tender gestures flow from the inward combustion of love that we have in our hearts. The Lord's love for us is described in this way:

> For God so loved the world that He gave His
> only begotten Son, that whosoever believeth
> in Him should not perish, but have everlasting
> life (St. John 3:16).

We know that He loves us by looking in faith at what He did for us. On the cross of Calvary, God literally expressed His love for humanity. There's something special about seeing your spouse sacrifice for you that gives you a greater appreciation and love for them. The sacrificial acts, the going out of their way, the extending of themselves, speak a language that communicates directly with our heart. In addition to these gestures, we express love to our spouse sexually. Having sex with your spouse is not just about you getting your needs met, it's also about you meeting the needs of your spouse and the mutual giving of your bodies to accomplish that.

We believe that the Bible is the inspired Word of God. In it, we learn about God's redemption plan for the lost and how salvation is through the sacrificial death and glorious resurrection of Jesus Christ. It reveals to us His heart and what He desires for mankind. From the scriptures, we learn about creation, sin, human behavior, salvation, God's expectations, eternity, etc. Interestingly, we don't see in the scriptures a "how to manual" when it comes to sex. Although we read in the Song of Solomon of what appears to be marital sex described with beautiful imagery (Chapter 4), you can't go to a verse of scripture where it's spelled out step by step. Why is that? With something so pivotal to the human experience and its continuance as sex, you would think that God would have elaborated in detail on the subject. We do have in Genesis 1:27–28, God's command to the first man Adam to "be fruitful and multiply" but as for how to go about doing that, the scriptures don't say.

I glean from the lack of scriptural instructions, that God desires a husband and wife to embark on a joyous journey of experiencing each other through an interchange of intimate expressions of touching, caressing, kissing, and deeply gazing into each other's eyes. They are to grow together, becoming freer to comfortably express their love, losing inhibition and reservation. To me, the lack of scriptural instruction implies for there to be searching and mystery as husband and wife explore together the adventure of lovemaking and learn to interpret each other's signals. Like a facial expression can demonstrate inner emotions, a couple's offering of their bodies to each other in sexual integrity and purity reveals the exclusivity of their love. Human sexuality is a way that we express ourselves to the one that we've vowed to love for a lifetime. We are sexual beings with urges and yearnings for sexual gratification and should understand that God has ordained marriage as the outlet for those desires to be expressed and fulfilled.

For a husband and wife that are newly married, their sexual experiences may initially have awkwardness. This is normal and a part of the "becoming one" process as they learn each other's rhythm and pleasure points. Over time, they develop chemistry, a depth of knowledge of one another, and like a symphony, they build to a crescendo of release and delight; God has designed it to be so. When they're done, there's no guilt or shame because they have God's approval on their union and lovemaking.

I see an interesting similarity between making cement and lovemaking. The making of cement includes gathering raw materials that go through a process of crushing, pre-homogenization, storing, heating, etc. The process prepares the mixture to be poured, where it will sit, settle, and solidify. Likewise, the making of love involves the collecting of the raw materials of our essence, which will also be going through the process of becoming one. We pour ourselves into each other, blending our spirit, soul, and body in a love exchange that reveals our passion and commitment to each other. The sexual intercourse between husband and wife helps the relationship to sit, settle, and become stronger.

The sexual experience in marriage is ordained by God to further strengthen, tighten, and seal the couple in a lifetime union. The scriptures tell us that,

> Marriage should be honored by all, and the marriage bed kept pure, for God will judge the adulterer and all the sexually immoral (Hebrews 13:4 NIV).

Marriage is an institution of honor to be respected and carefully entered. Other means of sexual gratification are condemned by God and those that engage in it have the promise of judgment to look forward to. Why is sex outside of marriage considered a sin by God? If a man and woman are not married, but consenting, and want to be together sexually, why is that an issue with God? These are good questions that deserve our attention.

When you have sex outside of marriage, you're engaging in that which God has reserved for those that have entered covenant relationship, pledging lifetime commitment. You are engaging in the cementing process without the commitment to be joined. The beauty of sex is cheapened when it is outside of the marital union. The way that God has provided for sexual relations to be experienced is in marriage, between two people that are one in His eyes. By looking at marriage, you should see God's unwavering commitment and love for the church. A man loving, honoring, and cherishing his wife pictures the love Christ has for the church. He has obligated Himself to love and care for the church forever. Having sex is meant to be the outward gesture that displays our inward commitment that we belong exclusively to each other. God did not design sex to be between boyfriend and girlfriend, or for those playing house. It's not for people that meet and feel a strong attraction for each other. Sex within marriage is God's wedding gift to the couple where they can express their love and life-long commitment to each other in the most intimate way.

SECTION 4: LASTING

Lasting

Your marriage is meant to be meaningful, enjoyable, and for life. Unfortunately, a mindset exists today that is more concerned about the moment, with little to no thought about the long term. There is much emphasis being placed on loyalty, where people want loyalty in their relationships, from family, friends, coworkers, and so on. Even in professional sports, fans want their favorite players to be loyal to the city and to play out their contracts without abandoning the local team. Many want loyalty but may not necessarily be equipped to be loyal themselves. We've grown accustomed to seeing bad break-ups, divorces, the end of friendships, and many other relationships being terminated.

In this closing section of the book, I want to look at the materials that are necessary to build a marriage that will last for a lifetime. We will be challenged to honor God, uphold our vows, and commit to a life of sacrificial love. As we view marriage from a standpoint of permanence, possibilities, and pleasure, God will reveal to us His purpose. Concerning love, the Word says,

> it bears all things, believes all things, hopes all things, endures all things. Love never fails – 1

Cor. 13:7-8. (NKJV)

X. GOOFY TOGETHER

"JUST LIKE DRUNKENNESS INFLU-
ENCES THE DRINKER'S BEHAVIOR,
SO TOO, LOVE IN MARRIAGE LEADS
YOU TO SWEETNESS, JOYFULNESS,
AND LAUGHTER."

A common issue that we have as Christians endeavoring to win people to Christ is getting them to see how our faith is relevant and is not just an outdated religion. Many feel that the Bible is no longer adequate to relate to the things we're experiencing in our "modern times." As a result, the church is placed on mute, and the world would rather hear from the so-called experts and the TV talking heads of the day. If only we could get them to understand the joy that we've come to know in serving the Lord; if only we could find the words to express the delight, we have in being saved and the benefits of having God Himself ordering our steps through this maze of life. Although we may not always have the words to say, we can live the kind of life that speaks to them in a way they can't deny.

Unfortunately, some in the Christian faith come across as stuffed shirts with a pompous demeanor. Without a doubt, we are living in challenging times, and marriages are being tested; this demands seriousness from us about life. But even as we face tough times, we can do it with the joy of the Lord which is our strength. Our marriages will be strengthened when we really appreciate and celebrate love. The bliss, the singing, and the laughter that we experienced on the day of our wedding don't have to be a distant memory only to be visited in our mind or when we look at pictures. The elapsing of time should never diminish the love that we share within our marriage. On your wedding day, you made the choice to be joined to your spouse. During your marriage, you can choose to walk daily in the abundant life that the Lord said He came to give us. Jesus said,

> the thief cometh not, but for to steal, and to kill, and to destroy; I am come that they might have life, and that they might have it more abundantly. (St. John 10:10).

Real living is not in accumulating as much money and materialistic things as you can; it's in enjoying the riches of God's grace. He intends for love to be celebrated throughout the years of your marriage.

> May your fountain be blessed, and may you rejoice in the wife of your youth. A loving doe, a graceful deer- may her breasts satisfy you always, may you ever be intoxicated with her love. Proverbs 5:18-19.

Notice the poetic words that describe how enraptured the husband should be, under the influence of love. Just like drunkenness influences the drinker's behavior, so too, love in marriage leads you to sweetness, joyfulness, and laughter. A woman that is showered by the love of her husband and is spoken to by him with words that her heart longs to hear will shine with a radiance that pours forth from the depths of her being. A man that is encouraged and loved by his wife will have an inner satisfaction that he will proudly wear on his face. This is very noticeable to people around them; family, friends, and even strangers will recognize that you are filled with joy and excitement. That becomes a part of your testimony, and many will want to have the same joy that they see in your marriage.

There's a misconception that people have about God, where they understand Him to be a grumpy old man in the heavens waiting to pounce on those that disobey Him. He is often believed to be an angry God with a set of rules that you better not disobey. We acknowledge that yes, God is a holy and righteous God. He does require of us obedience to His Word and for us to forsake our sinful ways, but that only describes an aspect of our infinite God. He is also loving, merciful, patient, and kind. In seeking to understand God, we should consider what He put in us to comprehend how He wants our experience in life and marriage to be. He made us with senses like taste, touch, seeing, hearing, and smelling, which are five of the basics among many others. These senses help us to connect to the physical world. There's also sense of humor within us, which is the ability to laugh and experience outbursts of joy. So, His Word tells us, "A merry heart doeth good like a medicine: but a broken spirit drieth the bones." (Proverbs 17:22).

It's interesting to me that the servant of the Lord, Moses, gave instruction to God's people that when a man first gets married, he was not to go to war or to be charged with any duties, but he shall be free at home one year and shall cheer up his wife (Deuteronomy 24:5). Simply stated, this command was given to prevent the man from being away from his new bride, and to ensure that there would be nothing to cause him to be absent from his home so that he could literally "brighten her up." For a year they would be free to joyfully express and celebrate their love. The challenge for married couples is to maintain joyful marriages, even though there will be difficult things to face. Having an ability to laugh together makes a difference. When you have a merry heart, it releases preserving, restorative properties that are beneficial to our bodies and invigorates our marriages.

Some of the most side-splitting laughs that I've had were with my wife. I'm talking about the kind of laugh where you cry tears and drip snot. We've enjoyed laughs together where she laughs until it turns into a snorting sound, and the sound of my laughter momentarily goes away and then comes back with a roar. Have you ever noticed that you and your spouse will have a great laugh to-gether, but when you share the story or thing that made you laugh with someone else; it didn't come across quite as funny? That's because God has given you and your spouse that special something be-tween you because of the love you share, and that certain uniqueness that is tailored to your married experience, only the two of you can really appreciate your goofiness. It's not always meant to be shared with others; no matter how funny the both of you think it is. It's especially designed for your enjoyment and becomes a memory that brings delight to your heart whenever you think of it. You may not be able to relate the funny moments you share together as a couple to others, but the joy that flows from you will be evidenced in your marriage.

There's something refreshing about a good laugh. Being a big kid at heart, I love to make my wife laugh, chasing her around the house, tickling her. Being silly together has a certain youthful quality about it and helps you to enjoy each other even more. Love is exciting, and love is joyous. You should be enthralled and intoxicated by it. Others should see your exuberance and the delight you have in each other. Our children, who are both young, blush when they see our goofy displays of affection, but it teaches them. It lets them see the great pleasure that their mommy and daddy find in each other. Whenever my wife and I embrace, like clockwork, our girls run to join in and make a love circle—family hug. It's because love and laughter are inviting; we all want to be a part of it.

XI. LAYERS AND PRAYERS

"BEING ABLE TO HAVE HEART-
TO-HEART CONVERSATIONS,
EVEN ABOUT YOUR STRUGGLES
AND ISSUES, IS A FOUNDATIONAL
BUILDING BLOCK FOR HAVING A
STRONG MARRIAGE."

W e describe things that are difficult as being like "pulling teeth." Over the years, as I have counseled with couples and individuals, one thing that I find is a struggle for people is for them to open and discuss matters of the heart, their deep-seated fears, and those things that instigate inner turmoil. Years of not being able to articulate on uncomfortable subjects and talking through sensitive issues can cause you to retreat behind a self-constructed wall, warding off all attempts to probe and understand you. As a result, much of the problems that your spouse is faced with are trying to conquer the obstacle course that you've set up to protect yourself. When confronted with the options, (1) walk through a painful process with your spouse to healing or (2) hide behind walls, it's no surprise when the easier route is taken. The problem however is that barricading yourself behind walls and under layers only prevents intimacy and your spouse from truly getting to know you.

How well do you know your spouse? Not the information that their coworker may know or things that the neighbor could tell you. I'm not asking about their favorite color or favorite movie; I'm speaking about those inward qualities and inherent characteristics, their motivations and the things that drive them. What about their fears and regrets? Do you understand their history and the road they've travelled that contributed to why they think the way that they do? Does that even interest you? Another set of important questions to ponder is how well you will allow your spouse to know you, and do you keep secrets from your spouse? The level of intimacy and transparency in your marriage is determined by you and your spouse. Do you want a relationship that is honest, where the two of you can delve into the depths of one another without judgment or holding things against each other? These are important questions that we should very much be interested in answering sincerely. As married couples, we travel through life encountering a range of things, from health issues, money matters, to family life crises. We see the birth of our children and share in all their growing pains. We go through times of hardship and difficulty, sometimes shedding tears. As we face these ordeals, our character and true self is revealed. Allowing yourself to be vulnerable to your spouse is not a sign of weakness, but it is a sign of strength. Unfortunately, the thought is "If I allow myself to be exposed to my spouse, at some point it will be used against me." Sadly, it often is, but that is not what marriage should be.

There are things that people hide in marriages like money, secret children, affairs, and porn addiction, but there are also those scars and intrinsic things that have to do with your past that are often hidden as well. You should see your spouse as your confidant; the person that you want to talk to when you need to be heard and understood; the one that you're sure will listen and correctly interpret the palpitations of your hurting heart. If you are reading this and saying within yourself that you can't confide in your spouse that way, then maybe this would be a great topic to discuss with your spouse, expressing your desire for that type of relationship. Being able to have heart-to-heart conversations, even about your struggles and issues, is a foundational building block for having a strong marriage.

To really get to the crux of those types of things, it's necessary to penetrate through the layers that some in marriages hide behind to create a safe place, not understanding that God ordained marriage to be the safe place. Your marriage should be a retreat from bad intentions, selfish motives, and negativity; those things should not describe what we present to each other. Within each of our hearts is a place that is reserved for God alone, where He is to rule as our King, Lord, and Savior. When He has that place in our heart, He not only has access to you, but also to your spouse through you. Just think of it, as you love your spouse, God works in conjunction with you to pull you both closer to His heart. God's love can penetrate the thickest walls and melt the hardest of hearts; and you are instrumental in Him accomplishing that as it relates to your spouse.

A practical step to take, that will help couples experience deeper intimacy, is to spend time together praying. This probably sounds strange to some to suggest that engaging in something spiritual like prayer would result in greater intimacy, so let's look. Prayer presents an opportunity to go before the Lord in surrender, acknowledging your need for His help and guidance; it's where we call on Him to give us strength and salvation and all the things that He can do that set Him apart as God. Prayer is a privilege where our heart can commune with Him and have our fears allayed. Prayer invokes His presence, and He hovers over us like a mother bird warmly sits on her eggs to incubate them. He alone sees us as we truly are, so when we sincerely approach Him in prayer, jointly unburdening our hearts, like a master seamstress, He sews our hearts together. In our tears, and crying out to Him, all barriers and stony exteriors begin to melt away. In raw, graphic truth, we see each other's vulnerabilities and become even more inspired to love unconditionally. It's His love working through us that enables us to love that way. The more that a husband and wife commit to praying together, the more comfortable they will be doing it; and the stronger their bond will be.

* * *

God knows each of us. Every hidden secret, beyond the layers, and between the crevices of our heart; God is infinitely aware of every detail of our lives. Even the things that we aren't conscious of concerning ourselves don't escape from His all-seeing eyes. The Psalmist understood this and wrote:

You have searched me, Lord, and you know

me. You know when I sit and when I rise; you perceive my thoughts from afar. You discern my going out and my lying down; you are familiar with all my ways. Before a word is on my tongue you, Lord, know it completely (Psalm 139:1–4).

His knowledge of us makes Him an endless stream of wisdom that flows into our hearts, enlightening us about ourselves, our mate, and what we can do to be more sensitive to one another's needs.

XII. HEIRS TOGETHER
(THE FORGIVENESS FACTOR)

"IT'S A STRUGGLE FOR MANY IN THEIR MARRIAGE TO MOVE PAST AN OFFENSE, AND IT USUALLY BECOMES A MENTAL STRONG-HOLD THAT DOMINATES YOUR THOUGHTS, HOLDING YOU CAP-TIVE."

Being in ministry has afforded me the opportunity to provide pastoral counseling to people where I hear the many questions and concerns that come from hurting hearts. One of the subjects that comes up most often has to do with forgiveness—the need to forgive and be forgiven. Also, there are many that struggle to forgive themselves. The whole Christian faith rests on a foundation of God forgiving us through the work of Christ on the cross of Calvary. We can be forgiven because Christ took our place, dying for our sins, and when we believe in Him, God washes away all our sins.

In our relationships, we may offend each other. We say things, we do things, and we fail to do things; these ultimately hurt someone. Marriage can expose you to hurts because of the nature of it. In that, we are in a relationship that involves trust, disclosure, our feelings and matters of the heart, there's the potential to be injured. When that happens and you experience a hurt at the hands of your spouse, the need for forgiveness is presented. When someone that you love hurts you, it hurts worse. It doesn't just hurt being on the receiving end of an offense, but it should hurt just as much knowing that there are times when we are the offenders. Of course, we don't want to hurt anyone or be on the receiving end, but it especially hurts when it comes from your spouse because it's where your heart resides, and the hurtful act is contradictory to the love that you share. Some actions can be to the level that they make you question the love, and in some cases, it contributes to the demise of the marriage.

We know that the goal of our Christian walk is to become more like Christ. After our new birth in Him by the work of His Spirit, our mind is renewed, and we are transformed through the process of sanctification. In becoming like Christ, we are to practice forgiveness and show mercy. What exactly is forgiveness and what does it look like in our marriages? Forgiveness is the act of releasing someone from something that they owe or the cancellation of a debt. In 1Peter 3:7, the apostle mentions that husbands and wives are heirs together of the grace of life. I see in that portion of scripture the need for agreement and understanding that together they are recipients of God's grace. As heirs together, we literally have inherited the riches of coexisting in God's favor and love. Husband, when you realize that your wife needs God's grace; and wife, when you accept that your husband needs the Savior; it reduces the judgement and raises the appreciation for His grace toward you. When we acknowledge that we both fall short, and miss the mark, then we can be better positioned to extend forgiveness to each other. When we equally exhibit a "merciful mindset" and have a "pardoning perspective" toward each other in marriage, it brings healing and sweetness. This is not to say that we gloss over when we've been wronged or that we ignore things that are offensive. Marriage is about open conversations and the ability to point out the things we don't like or the times we believe we were mishandled, but we should also agree that we won't allow issues to go unresolved, and we'll address them with empathy and grace. Our commitment is to God and to each other, and with that being the case; the goal is to exercise forgiveness.

It's a struggle for many in their marriage to move past an offense, and it usually becomes a mental stronghold that dominates your thoughts, holding you captive. Even when a person moves toward forgiving, genuinely desiring to release the offender, the offense may still rear its ugly face, flashing through your mind. As a result, it initiates a drifting away from intimacy, slowly cooling your love and affection. There are some that have made the decision that they had to part ways because of what their spouse did to them, and divorce was the outcome. I would say to you, even in that case, forgiving is still necessary in that it releases you from the prison of anger and hostility. I have counseled with many people that have been scarred from marriages where they endured unfaithfulness, abandonment, abuse, and all kinds of hurtful things. The offender often moves on, sometimes even dies, and the person that they hurt is left struggling to overcome feelings of hate, anger, and resentment. All those feelings are fueled with the lingering memories of what was done to them. Forgiveness is the tool that you can wield to begin disconnecting yourself from the chains that burden your soul. Why should you carry the unbearable weight of someone else's wrong-doing? Forgiveness is the frame of mind that says, "I'll release the offender and the hurt they inflicted to God for Him to issue out what He deems to be appropriate without wishing harm or retribution." For others that have decided to forgive and stay married, they may be having great difficulty hurdling what was done to them and need God's help; especially when the thing that was done has ongoing consequences that stare you in the face. God's grace is sufficient to assist you in the forgiving (process). When you sincerely make the choice to forgive, God will give you grace daily to achieve it. The one that has done the wrong has a very important job to do. It's vital for them to bear the burden of responsibility for what they've done, giving their spouse that they have offended adequate time to sort through this challenge. What helps to initiate healing is when the offender asks their spouse for forgiveness, demonstrates contrition, and a change in the offensive behavior. Trust being restored may take some time; the offender needs to be patient and prepared for this possibility.

As little children, many of us learned what we call the Lord's Prayer. We said it at night, just before going to bed; we taught our children the verses, and they committed them to memory, but I wonder if we really paid attention to the words: Forgive us our debts, as we forgive our debtors (St. Matthew 6:12). The great lesson is that what we are most in need of from God, forgiveness, we are to grant to others. We ask Him to forgive us, as we forgive those that are indebted or have sinned against us. When it comes to marriage, a relationship that is established to be for a lifetime, forgiving needs to be an intricate part of it.

XIII. THE CENTERPIECE

"WITHIN OUR MARRIAGE, WE ARE
TO FAN THE SWEET FRAGRANCE
OF SACRIFICE AND LOVE, LIKE A
SET TABLE AT A WEDDING RECEP-
TION CREATES AN AURA OF LOVE."

The centerpiece is the item on a table or some type of display that sets the theme for an event. It is the most important part because it calls everyone's attention to it and speaks to the occasion. Simply stated, the centerpiece is the main thing to visually set the tone. The best centerpieces are somewhat contradictory; on the one hand, it should be simple, but at the same time, elegant. Christ Jesus dying on the cross over two thousand years ago was God's foreordained centerpiece that He set at the center of all human history, and what the Lord did on that cross demonstrated an unfathomable depth of love. Though it was a brutal event, it was also glorious in that it was accomplishing for us the means to have access to the Father. It was God's example to us of "sacrificial love."

As husbands and wives, we have specific roles and responsibilities that God has given us that will help us to experience a deeper level of love and commitment. Both husband and wife are to demonstrate sacrifice in how they relate to one another; it is our Lord's example on the cross. Loving sacrificially empties us of selfishness and causes there to be a love theme within the marriage. Within our marriage, we are to fan the sweet fragrance of sacrifice and love, like a set table at a wedding reception creates an aura of love. Being inspired to love by the example of Christ offering Himself to save us, our marriage should be decorated with actions of love and displays of kindness. God is the centerpiece that is to be set on the table of our lives, giving us a visual of the way that we should love our spouse.

His Word specifically lays out for us the roles of husbands and wives to help set the table and the trajectory for our marriage to take flight. Submission is the mission for wives. As we seek to understand what the Biblical idea of a wife submitting to her husband is, let's first understand what it is not. Submission for wives is not about a husband declaring to her, "I'm in charge; you have to do what I say." It's not about him being the boss. A wife submitting to her husband is about her obedience to God and adhering to what He has established to bless and benefit the marriage. Just like in the uniformed services, you have ranking officers with different levels of authority. It's not that the higher-ranking officer is better than those with lesser rank; it's simply that levels of authority and responsibility, are what give the operation cohesiveness and flow. A wife, who is equal to her husband, is to voluntarily choose to submit to him which will contribute to the success of her marriage. She's not inferior; she's just wisely investing in God's economy for a prosperous marriage.

For husbands, it's about headship. He is to be accountable to God for his home and marriage. He is to first know that Christ is his head, and that he must demonstrate submission to Him (See Ephesians 5:23). When Adam and Eve disobeyed God and ate the forbidden fruit, God came seeking for them in the garden, and although Eve was the first to eat the fruit, then giving it to her husband, God called

Adam into account first. Adam had to give an answer for what happened because he was the head of the home (Gen. 3:9). The husband being accountable doesn't relieve the wife of any responsibility; she also will answer for her actions as we saw with Eve whom God questioned second for what she had done (Gen. 3:13). The husband can help the wife with her role of submission by loving her the way that Christ loves the church. His love for us, who make up the church, was seen when He gave His life for us. Likewise, husbands are to give of themselves in three main aspects. He is to be the priest, protector, and provider of his home. As the priest of his home, he is the spiritual covering, receiving instructions from God to lead his family. As protector of his home, he is to shield his family, both spiritually and physically. As provider, he gives of himself to sustain and support his family. Even though his wife may be the breadwinner, making more money than he does, he is committed to his responsibility to make sure that the needs of his family are met.

When a couple is committed to honoring God as the focal point of their marriage, endeavoring to fulfill their roles, God obliges Himself to take them into the depths and dimensions of love. Love is simplistic, yet mysterious, difficult to find, but easy to recognize. When God is at the center of your relationship, you then have a target to aim at. Your spouse is your prayer partner, your best friend, and your biggest supporter. You are helpers; one to the other, submitting to God and to each other, walking through life's journey, and because God is at the center, He brings it all together. It's God that gives insight into your spouse, allowing you to see their needs, and He graces you with patience and understanding to care for them.

The discovery is ongoing and rewarding. We don't get to a place where we exhaust all that we can understand and know about each other. The beautiful thing about this discovery process called marriage is you become aware that God has placed keys in your spouse that unlock things in you. Your spouse helps you to know yourself better as God helps them to see in you the things that even you aren't aware of. As you both journey through the years of your marriage, converging at the center to meet God, along the way, you discover the meaning, the purpose and, the freshness of God's love in each other that will keep you together.

Acknowledgements

To my sisters, Rhonda and Robin, and their families,
Thank you for all your encouragement and suggestions.

To my New Covenant church family,
It is a privilege to serve you with the love of the Lord.

To Eldridge Rice for introducing me to Katrina,
You saw the potential of us being together, and although matchmaking wasn't your thing, you were persistent in your suggestions that we should meet. Oh, how right you were!

To all of you that will read the words of this book,
Whatever you are facing in your life, I pray that you will be greatly inspired to draw closer to God, who loves you and experience His love that shines down on us like the rays of the sun.

From the heart and hand of Reginald Reaves

ABOUT THE AUTHOR

Reginald Reaves

Reginald Reaves is fulfilling his life's assignment
to preach and teach God's
life changing Word, de-
livering insights to
strengthen families, in-
spire hope, and to pro-
claim salvation in Christ
to those that are lost. He
serves under the leader-
ship of his Dad, Bishop Alfred Reaves, the senior
Pastor of the Church of
the New Covenant in Bal-
timore, Maryland.

Pastor Reggie's ministry approach of finding answers to life's problems and challenges in God's

Word has brought healing and wise counsel to many. "God's Word is not an outdated, ancient book that is too old fashioned to speak to our modern issues; to the contrary, it has relevance and speaks directly to who we are and why we are."

Pastor Reggie is driven to see the rebuilding and restoration of families, and an ignition of faith in God. He holds a Bachelor of Ministry from International Seminary in Plymouth, Florida and is continuing his education in pastoral counseling and family studies.

He is married to the love of his life, Katrina Reaves, and together they serve in ministry endeavoring to bless their community, one family at a time. They are the proud parents of their two daughters, Brielle, and Thalia Reaves.

Made in the USA
Middletown, DE
11 September 2022